COUNTRIES OF THE WORLD

Singapore

Gareth Stevens Publishing

A WORLD ALMANAC EDUCATION GROUP COMPANY

JUL - - 2002

About the Authors: James Michael Baker is a teacher at the Singapore American School and author of *Crossroads: A History of Malaysia and Singapore*. Junia Marion Baker is editor of the Singapore American community newspaper. Both are U.S. citizens who have lived in Singapore for many years.

PICTURE CREDITS

American Club of Singapore: 82
Arkib Negara Malaysia: 10
Bes Stock: cover, 39 (top), 44, 65, 66
Canadian High Commission, Singapore: 79, 83, 84
Alain Evrard: 1, 3 (top), 27 (top), 31, 75
Globe Press: 4, 60
Jill Gocher: 45 (bottom)
Hans Hayden: 19 (top), 21 (bottom), 30, 32 (top), 32 (bottom), 40 (top), 41, 57 (top), 62
HBL Network Photo Agency: 3 (bottom), 7, 14, 19 (bottom), 53, 67, 71, 74
Bjorn Klingwall: 40 (bottom)
Kodak (Singapore) Pte. Limited: 77
Earl Kowall: 6, 9, 17, 20, 26, 27 (bottom), 28, 38, 39 (bottom), 47, 51, 52, 68, 69
Catherine Lim: 29 (bottom)
Gilles Massot: 8, 11, 56, 61
Ministry of Education Singapore: 22, 24, 25, 73
National Archives of Singapore: 12, 15 (top), 15 (center), 46, 48, 58, 72 (bottom), 81
National University of Singapore: 72 (top)
Christine Osborne Pictures: 18, 29 (top), 35, 49
Singapore American Newspaper: 85
Singapore National Olympic Council: 3 (center), 36 (top), 37
Singapore Tourism Board: 5, 21 (top), 33, 34, 36 (bottom), 42, 43, 45 (top), 50, 59, 70, 80, 87, 89, 91
Straits Times: 13, 15 (bottom), 16 (top), 54, 55, 76, 78
Yu Hui Ying: 2, 16 (bottom), 23, 57 (bottom), 64

Digital Scanning by Superskill Graphics Pte Ltd

Written by
JAMES MICHAEL BAKER AND JUNIA MARION BAKER

Edited by
SCOTT MARSH

Edited in the U.S. by
**PATRICIA LANTIER
MONICA RAUSCH**

Designed by
LYNN CHIN

Picture research by
SUSAN JANE MANUEL

First published in North America in 2002 by
Gareth Stevens Publishing
A World Almanac Education Group Company
330 West Olive Street, Suite 100
Milwaukee, Wisconsin 53212 USA

Please visit our web site at
www.garethstevens.com
For a free color catalog describing
Gareth Stevens' list of high-quality books
and multimedia programs, call
1-800-542-2595 (USA) or
1-800-461-9120 (CANADA).

Fax: (414) 332-3567.

© **TIMES MEDIA PRIVATE LIMITED 2002**
Originated and designed by
Times Editions
An imprint of Times Media Private Limited
A member of the Times Publishing Group
Times Centre, 1 New Industrial Road
Singapore 536196
http://www.timesone.com.sg/te

Library of Congress Cataloging-in-Publication Data
Baker, James Michael.
Singapore / by James Michael Baker and Junia Marion Baker.
p. cm. — (Countries of the world)
Includes bibliographical references and index.
Summary: Provides an overview of the geography, history, government, lifestyle, language, art, and food of Singapore, exploring its customs and current issues.
ISBN 0-8368-2346-X (lib. bdg.)
1. Singapore—Juvenile literature. [1. Singapore.] I. Baker, Junia Marion. II. Title. III. Countries of the world (Milwaukee, Wis.)
DS609.B35 2002
959.57—dc21 2001041155

Printed in Malaysia

1 2 3 4 5 6 7 8 9 06 05 04 03 02

Contents

AN OVERVIEW OF SINGAPORE

The Republic of Singapore is situated at the southern tip of the Malaysian peninsula. This tiny country has virtually no natural resources, and much of its fresh water is piped from Malaysia. Even basic food items, such as rice, have to be imported. Despite these disadvantages, Singapore's multicultural population has worked hard to turn the country into a modern-day success story. Today, Singapore enjoys the highest standard of living in Southeast Asia. Singapore's largest ethnic groups are Chinese, Malays, and Indians. A small portion of the population has mixed Asian and European ancestry. Once a small trading post, Singapore now has the busiest port in Southeast Asia and is one of the world's great commercial centers.

Opposite: Part of the Central Business District overlooks the Singapore River. The bridge in the foreground is Elgin Bridge, which was built in the 1920s.

Below: Shops selling everything from souvenirs to household items can be found throughout Singapore.

THE FLAG OF SINGAPORE

The flag of Singapore is red and white. A red band across the top half of the flag represents brotherhood and equality. A white band below it stands for virtue and purity. The red band contains a crescent moon and five stars. The crescent moon symbolizes the young nation, and the five stars stand for democracy, peace, progress, justice, and equality. The flag was first flown in December 1959, when Singapore became self-governing, except in matters of internal security, defense, and foreign affairs. The flag was officially adopted in 1965 when Singapore gained independence from Malaysia.

Geography

Singapore consists of one large island and 60 adjacent islands and has a total area of 255 square miles (660 square kilometers). The main island measures about 26 miles (42 kilometers) from east to west and 14 miles (23 km) from north to south. Singapore is located at the southern tip of Malaysia. The Johor Strait separates Singapore from Peninsular Malaysia. The South China Sea is to its west. The Singapore Strait to the south separates the islands of Indonesia and Singapore.

Land and Water

Singapore's longest river is the Seletar River, which is 10 miles (16 km) long. Many small streams flow through Singapore island and empty into the surrounding straits. Urban areas are drained by tree-lined concrete canals.

Singapore's coastline is mostly flat with a few cliffs that come down to the sea. Stretches of coastline have been modified by land reclamation work and the building of embankments.

LAND FROM THE SEA

Singapore relies on land reclamation to help ease the demands placed on its limited land area.
(A Closer Look, page 52)

Below: Despite the large extent of urbanization in Singapore, rural communities can still be found on some offshore islands. This small village is on Pulau Seking.

Singapore depends on Malaysia for about half of its water supply. The country hopes that building desalination plants will make Singapore less dependent on outside sources of water. Such plants remove salt from sea water so people can use the water.

Most of Singapore's land is low-lying, and it seldom rises more than 50 feet (15 meters) above sea level. The highest point is Bukit Timah Hill at 545 feet (166 m). Urbanized areas take up about half the country's land area, while 5 percent is covered with rain forest and mangrove swamps. The remaining land is made up of parks.

Singapore has about 5,782 acres (2,340 hectares) of parks, park connectors, and open spaces as well as more than 9,143 acres (3,700 ha) of roadside greenery and green state land. About forty species of trees thrive in Singapore.

The soil is primarily hard, red clay that is formed by laterization, or the sinking of nutrients far below the surface of the soil. Nevertheless, 2 percent of the land is arable. This land is used for growing fruit and vegetables for the local market and orchids for export.

Above: **Bukit Timah Nature Reserve in central Singapore has several nature trails that offer visitors a chance to relax after the hustle and bustle of city life.**

PARKS
Singapore has several nature reserves that offer visitors respite from the fast-paced urban lifestyle of Singapore.
(A Closer Look, page 56)

Climate

As Singapore lies just 85 miles (137 km) north of the equator, its temperature does not change much during the year. The average daily temperature ranges from 73° Fahrenheit (23° Celsius) to 93° Fahrenheit (34°C).

Singapore has two main seasons: the northeast monsoon from December to March and the southwest monsoon from June to September. These seasons are separated by two intermonsoonal periods called the presouthwest and prenortheast monsoons. The presouthwest monsoon lasts from April to May, and the prenortheast monsoon lasts from October to November. Although the northeast monsoon brings the most rain and cooler temperatures, rain falls throughout the year. On average, Singapore has 95 inches (241 centimeters) of rain each year.

Garden City

Singapore's wet and humid climate offers ideal conditions for tropical plants to grow. The country's plant life is lush and green throughout the year. More than three thousand species of tropical

Above: **The lush tropical climate of Singapore provides ideal conditions for orchids to flourish.**

plants grow in Singapore, mainly in mangrove swamps and the Bukit Timah Nature Reserve. Other areas with plenty of greenery are located near Singapore's reservoirs and in the Botanic Gardens.

Singapore has made an immense effort to keep its cityscape green and inviting to residents and visitors. The National Parks Board looks after Singapore's nature reserves, parks, and roadside greenery. The construction of park connectors will link major parks and nature sites to jogging and cycling tracks.

Singapore has seven hundred species of orchids, which grow easily in hot, humid climates. Other flowering plants, such as hibiscus, also thrive in this area. Common trees are tropical hardwoods, coconut, and mangroves. Some species, such as the common pulai and angsana trees, are native to the region. Others, such as the frangipanni and rain trees, were brought in from the Americas and adapted to Singapore's tropical environment.

Wildlife

Except for birds, frogs, and snakes, wildlife in Singapore is scarce. Some monkeys, especially the long-tailed macaque, and squirrels still thrive in the forested areas and nature reserves.

About 150 bird species, including parakeets and pigeons, live around the country's reservoirs and in the forests. About one hundred additional species of migratory birds, such as egrets and plovers, stop twice a year in Singapore. They favor freshwater mangrove swamps, which are a rich source of food. These birds migrate between southern countries, such as Australia, and northern countries, such as Russia.

Below: **Singapore Zoological Gardens is committed to animal conservation and houses many species, such as these zebras, in simulated natural habitats.**

9

History

The Town by the Sea

Much of Singapore's early history is shrouded in legend and secondhand accounts. Chinese sailors in the twelfth to fourteenth centuries described Singapore as a pirate's lair. The island was once named *Temasek* (tuh-MAH-sek), which means "sea town." The Sanskrit name *Singapura* (SING-ah-POO-rah), meaning "lion city," was more commonly used by the end of the fourteenth century. Archaeological evidence indicates that the island was part of a Malay kingdom during the thirteenth and fourteenth centuries. It was ruled by a prince from Sumatra named Parameswara.

Raffles and the British

Modern Singapore was founded in 1819 by an Englishman, Sir Thomas Stamford Raffles. At the time, Britain's interests in the East were represented by the East India Company (EIC). Raffles, who worked for the EIC, struck a deal with the territorial chief of Johor to appoint a king who was friendly to the British. This king then turned Singapore over to the EIC.

The EIC ruled Singapore until 1867. The company was interested mainly in making profits and did little to improve living conditions in Singapore. Although the port prospered,

RAFFLES OUTWITS THE DUTCH

Singapore was actually a colony under Dutch control when Sir Thomas Stamford Raffles began his search for a British base in Southeast Asia.
(A Closer Look, page 58)

Below: Orang Laut (OH-rahng LAH-oat), or sea gypsies, lived on houseboats and were part of Singapore's small population when Raffles first arrived.

10

the people faced serious problems of lawlessness. Singapore's early immigrants from China were dominated by gangs, or "secret societies." Problems such as gambling became widespread.

A Crown Colony

In 1867, the British government took over Singapore from the EIC. It ruled Singapore as part of the Straits Settlements, which included Singapore, Penang, and Malacca. Advances in steamship design and the opening of the Suez Canal in 1869 dramatically increased the volume of trade between Europe and Asia. Singapore was well-placed to benefit from this trade because of its central location. At the end of the nineteenth century, the growth of the rubber and tin industries in Malaya (now Malaysia) and oil industry in Indonesia added to Singapore's importance.

Singapore provided banking and commercial services for traders throughout the area, as well as the complete servicing of ships and cargo. Some products were taken off small boats and put on steamships. Other products, such as tin and oil, were refined in Singapore before being shipped out. By the turn of the twentieth century, Singapore was the seventh largest port in the world.

Above: **This statue of Sir Thomas Stamford Raffles was erected in 1972 along the banks of the Singapore River. The statue's location is believed to be the spot where Raffles first landed in Singapore in 1819.**

IMMIGRANTS: THEN AND NOW

Singapore has attracted many immigrants throughout its history.
(A Closer Look, page 48)

The Great Depression and World War II

Two important turning points in Singapore's history were the worldwide economic depression in the 1930s and the Japanese occupation during World War II. During the Great Depression, the colonial government feared a sudden rush of male foreigners looking for work. The government restricted Chinese male, but not female, immigration. As more females settled in Singapore, more Chinese began to intermarry and raise families. Many Singaporeans date their ties to the country from this time.

The Japanese occupation of the island from 1942 to 1945 showed Singapore's immigrant population that Britain was no longer an invincible world power. After British forces in Singapore surrendered to the Japanese in 1942, many Allied prisoners of war and Asians endured years of great hardship. This experience led to the desire for self-rule among Singapore's Asian residents.

Self-Rule and Independence

After the war, the British returned to Singapore. They wanted to make Peninsular Malaya independent but keep Singapore as a colony. They felt Singapore was the key to rebuilding their economic interests in the region and that it would be an extremely important military base.

Above: Although Singaporeans initially welcomed the return of the British after World War II, they soon wanted their colonial rulers out of the country.

THE JAPANESE OCCUPATION

The Japanese occupied Singapore for three-and-a-half years during World War II. This occupation by an Asian power showed Singapore's Asian residents that European powers were not invincible. The realization led to demands for self-rule after the British returned to Singapore at the end of the war.

(A Closer Look, page 50)

Most Singaporeans, however, wanted to decide their own future at that time, especially after Singapore was split from the other Straits Settlements in 1946. Frequent demonstrations took place in the 1950s as locals wanted the British to hand over political power.

The first step toward independence took place in 1955, when Singaporeans voted for their first elected government. David Saul Marshall became Singapore's first locally-elected chief minister. He fought hard for total independence but resigned in 1956 when the British did not agree to his terms. Lim Yew Hock was Singapore's next chief minister. He continued to fight for more local control and negotiated the creation of the State of Singapore. The first elections under this new arrangement were held in 1959. The People's Action Party (PAP), led by Lee Kuan Yew, swept into power and has led the country since then.

Singapore became independent from Britain in 1963, when the country joined the Federation of Malaya — Malaya had been independent since 1957 — to create the new country of Malaysia. This union, however, was short-lived. Singapore was expelled from Malaysia in 1965 because both countries disagreed over several issues. That year, the independent Republic of Singapore was established.

TENSIONS ROCK THE FEDERATION

Singapore's entry into the Federation of Malaya was short-lived. Singapore's Chinese leadership and the Malay-led government of the federation did not agree on many issues. They clashed repeatedly over economic policies and the rights of the immigrant Chinese and Indians versus those of the indigenous Malays.

Left: On the shoulders of his supporters, Goh Chok Tong celebrates his reelection as Member of Parliament for Marine Parade in the 1988 elections. In 1990, Goh succeeded Lee Kuan Yew as prime minister.

WOMEN IN SINGAPORE

Singaporean women have made much progress in the struggle for women's rights.
(*A Closer Look*, page 72)

The Struggle for Success

The future did not look good for this new country with few natural resources and a multicultural population. When the British closed their military bases in 1971, Singapore was also left without a defense force. The population boom of the 1940s and 1950s had created housing and unemployment problems. Violence and tensions among Singapore's various races, or ethnic groups, rocked the country in the mid-1960s. The government needed to forge a common national identity for the country's diverse peoples. The government also faced frequent labor strikes in the 1960s.

Singapore has made tremendous progress since 1965. Its government mobilized Singaporeans to accept change and gave them the tools for success, such as education and up-to-date resources. Singapore was built by a hardworking society willing to sacrifice some of its personal interests to create a stable and prosperous nation. The country was able to take advantage of its location and offer vital services as Southeast Asia developed. In many ways, the national identity of modern Singaporeans comes from the pride they take in their accomplishments.

READY TO MOBILIZE

Singapore's armed forces are one of the best equipped militaries in the region. All men are required to serve for up to two-and-a-half years in National Service after completing high school.
(A Closer Look, page 60)

Below: Day or night, Singapore's Central Business District is always a hive of activity.

Elizabeth Choy (1910–)

Elizabeth Choy came to Singapore from British North Borneo in 1929 to train as a teacher. When the Japanese occupied Singapore in World War II, Choy was tortured and imprisoned for 193 days. They suspected her of helping Allied agents sabotage Japanese ships. In 1946, she was awarded the Order of the British Empire (OBE) for heroism during the war. In 1951, she became the only woman nominated to the Colonial Legislative Council, which was the highest local decision-making body at the time. She taught in several Singapore schools and became the first principal of the School for the Blind in 1956. In 1973, Choy was given the Long-Service Medal for her dedication to the teaching profession.

Elizabeth Choy

Yusof bin Ishak (1910–1970)

Yusof bin Ishak was born in Perak, Malaya, and came to Singapore as a child. He established the *Utusan Melayu*, a newspaper that became the voice of the Malay community. He was committed to racial equality and education for all. In 1959, when the colony was granted limited self-rule, Ishak became its first Malayan-born head of state, or Yang di-Pertuan Negara. In 1965, he became Singapore's first president. Ishak's determination to bring honor and prestige to Singapore set an impressive example for the country's future leaders to follow.

Yusof bin Ishak

David Saul Marshall (1908–1995)

David Saul Marshall was one of the founding fathers of Singapore. His Jewish ancestors came to Singapore from Baghdad in the mid-nineteenth century. He was a brilliant lawyer and public speaker who inspired many Singaporeans to join the struggle for independence. In 1955, Marshall became chief minister of Singapore's first elected government. That year, he led a mission to London to fight for Singapore's full independence. He was unsuccessful. After a second mission in 1956 failed, he resigned as Singapore's chief minister and founded the Workers' Party in 1957. He was Singapore's ambassador to France from 1978 to 1993. Marshall was widely regarded as one of Singapore's greatest criminal lawyers. Throughout his life, he was known for his humanity, compassion, and sense of fair play.

David Saul Marshall

Government and the Economy

The Republic of Singapore has a parliamentary system of government. However, since the country is a city-state and does not have state or county governments, the national government takes an active role in municipal matters. The president is elected by popular vote and holds office for six years. He or she has the power to veto appointments of public officials and government budgets. The president also advises Parliament on internal security matters and heads a council on minority rights. Singapore's current president, S. R. Nathan, was elected in 1999.

Singapore's Parliament has only one chamber, or house. Every citizen over the age of twenty-one must vote. Members of Parliament (MPs) are elected by popular vote. The cabinet is led by the prime minister, a member of Parliament who represents the majority party. Other ministers are appointed by the president on the advice of the prime minister. The cabinet is responsible for all government policies and administration.

LEE KUAN YEW

As prime minister of Singapore from 1959 to 1990, Lee Kuan Yew (*above*) led the country through some of its darkest days.
(A Closer Look, page 54)

Left: **The new Singapore Parliament House was completed in 1999. Built next to the old Parliament House, the premises consist of three new buildings and a restored building, which was formerly the Attorney General's Chambers.**

Although more than twenty political parties exist in Singapore, the PAP has led the government since independence in 1965. Singapore's current prime minister, Goh Chok Tong, came into office in 1990.

Government and the People

The government of Singapore places great importance on housing, education, and social welfare. Employers and employees contribute monthly payments to the Central Provident Fund (CPF), a savings and retirement program. Individuals may use their CPF savings for medical expenses and borrow against them to purchase an apartment or pay for university education.

Schools and public-service organizations, such as clinics and child care centers, receive grants and other benefits from the government. The government works with private community organizations through the Ministry of Community Development. This ministry oversees volunteer welfare organizations and promotes the concept of a caring and active community.

Above: Office and residential buildings often exist side by side in areas called housing estates. The residential building in the background was built under the country's public housing program.

JUDICIAL SYSTEM

Singapore law is based on English common law. The Supreme Court and subordinate courts represent the judicial power in the country. A Singapore Court of Appeal is the final court. Muslim religious or matrimonial affairs are handled by the *Syariah* (SHAH-ree-ah) Court.

The Economy

The economy of Singapore has grown rapidly since the country gained independence in 1965. Its gross domestic product (GDP) has grown at an average annual rate of about 8 percent since 1965. Brisk economic growth and low inflation rates have made Singapore one of the richest countries in the world.

When Singapore first attained independence, unemployment was a serious problem. Many people were also poorly educated. To create jobs for the people, the government attracted foreign investments in labor-intensive industries. By the early 1970s, unemployment rates had fallen. The government began to focus on economic activities that were more skill- and capital-intensive.

During an economic slowdown in the mid-1980s, economic activities carried out in Singapore were diversified. Consequently, Singapore became more active in the business and financial service sectors.

Today, Singapore is a global hub for manufacturing, finance, and communications. The country has built on the traditional strengths of its location, its hardworking people, and its role as a commercial and financial service center for the region.

Above: **Situated at the crossroads of international trade, the ports of Singapore are among the busiest in the world.**

Although its economy is more diverse, manufacturing is still the largest sector in the economy. It accounted for about 25 percent of the country's GDP in 1999. Other major areas of economic activity are commerce, business, transportation and communications, finance, and construction.

The government has also invested large sums of money toward developing a world-class infrastructure. For example, the ports of Singapore and Changi International Airport offer world-class services and facilities. The country is also the world's fourth largest banking and financial center, after New York, London, and Tokyo. International rating agencies consistently rank Singapore as one of the most competitive economies in the world. Singapore is also a regional or global hub for many multinational corporations.

Singapore is planning carefully for the future. The government has recognized the need to shift into knowledge-based economic activities. The country's information technology (IT) capabilities are being strengthened by its encouragement of high-technology business ventures. The education system has also been changed to encourage young Singaporeans to become creative and innovative thinkers. These steps are all intended to help Singapore remain competitive in the new millennium.

TOURISM

The tourism industry (*above*) is one of the largest sectors of Singapore's economy.
(*A Closer Look, page 66*)

Below: **Singapore Airlines is one of the busiest — and most profitable — airlines in the world.**

People and Lifestyle

Singapore has three main ethnic groups: Chinese, Malay, and Indian. Chinese make up about 77 percent of the population. Malays represent about 14 percent and Indians about 8 percent. Singaporeans of other ethnic groups, including about ten thousand Eurasians, make up the balance. Almost one million foreigners also live and work in Singapore.

Quality of Life

The United Nations human development index, which is based on income, life expectancy, and education, ranks Singapore among the top ten countries in the world. Almost everyone has a home with a television, telephone, and air-conditioning. Many Singaporeans also have computers and Internet access. The public transportation system is superb. Utilities and waste disposal systems are state of the art. Government services, such as the postal system, are also very efficient.

TRADITIONAL BELIEFS

Although Singapore is a modern society, many of its residents still believe in ancient superstitions.
(*A Closer Look, page 68*)

AGING POPULATION

Singapore has a low birthrate, and the number of retired people soon will exceed the number of people working. By 2020, there will be 117 retirees for every 100 workers.

HOUSING FOR THE PEOPLE
The government of Singapore launched a massive public housing program in the 1960s to relieve overcrowding and improve overall living conditions.
(*A Closer Look, page 46*)

Left: Many parents have busy work schedules, so family outings are treasured occasions.

Singaporeans work very hard. A forty-four hour workweek is the norm, although it is not unusual for employees to work much longer hours. The country's unemployment rate stands at 3.2 percent. Fifty-seven percent of the population is employed. About 56 percent of the women in Singapore work, a higher percentage than in any other Southeast Asian country. Over 75 percent of married women have jobs and juggle child care and housekeeping.

There are about 13,000 people per square mile (2.59 square km) in Singapore. About 86 percent of the population live in high-rise apartments built by the Housing and Development Board (HDB). These residential areas, known as housing estates, also have shops and offices. Thousands of people live in each housing estate and lead a busy, community-oriented lifestyle. The HDB is continuously upgrading older estates by adding new facilities, such as exercise areas.

The government offers programs that make home ownership possible for all citizens. Special programs also make it easier for different generations of families to live close to one another. The remainder of Singaporeans own private apartments or houses, while a small number rent their homes.

Above: **Singaporeans enjoy celebrating festive occasions with family and friends.**

Below: **Multimedia booths line Orchard Road, the main shopping district. These booths offer shoppers information, such as the location of the latest sale.**

Marriage

Many Chinese Singaporeans celebrate marriages with a formal tea ceremony. The newlyweds serve tea to their parents as a sign of respect. Chinese often celebrate a wedding with a huge banquet for their relatives and friends.

The Malay wedding ceremony is known as the *akad nikah* (AH-kahd NEE-kah). The akad nikah is a verbal contract between the groom and the bride's father. At the end of the ceremony, the groom gives his wife a *mas kahwin* (MAHS KAH-win). This is a small sum of money given to complete the wedding ceremony.

In Hindu wedding rituals, the brother-in-law of the bride places a ring on the bride's toe to symbolize the groom's promise to be faithful. The groom's parents hold the couple's hands while the bride's parents bless the union with holy water. This custom symbolizes that the groom's parents have endorsed his promises.

Christians formalize their vows in a church and celebrate afterward. Celebrations can be simple events or elaborate banquets and may include some Chinese or Hindu customs to please older family members who may not be Christian.

Above: Traditional Malay wedding ceremonies are colorful affairs.

THE STRAITS CHINESE

Peranakans (puh-RAH-nah-KAHNS) are a group of Straits Chinese whose ancestors intermarried with Malays to create a unique culture.
(*A Closer Look*, page 64)

CIVIL MARRIAGES

All couples are required by law to exchange their vows at the Registry of Marriages or the Registry of Muslim Marriages.

Children

Many Singaporean women continue working after giving birth; therefore, Singaporean parents have to consider how having children will affect their lives. Many Singaporean couples depend on others to help look after their children. Many rely on older relatives. Other couples hire maids or take their children to child care centers. The birthrate tends to be higher among Malays and Indians and lower in Chinese families. Since many families have only one or two children, the birth of a child is a special occasion.

Children are considered the inheritors of a greater Singapore. They might be spoiled and adored, but they are also pressured to succeed from a very young age. They are expected to excel at school and often receive private tutoring to improve their grades.

Family life tends to emphasize quality over quantity. In many families, both parents work. Children usually spend their days and sometimes weekday nights with maids or grandparents. When their parents are free on weekends, the entire family shops, catches up on household chores, and enjoys leisure activities together.

MULTITIERED FAMILIES

Multitiered families are common in Singapore. In a multitiered family, several generations of family members live in the same house. For example, many grandparents live with their married children and help raise the grandchildren.

Below: **Although they are usually pampered, a lot of pressure is placed on young Singaporeans to succeed academically.**

Education

Singapore has a very high standard of education. Singaporeans see education as a key to success. Consequently, many people continue to upgrade their skills throughout their lives.

Elementary school lasts for six years and is compulsory for all children. Although many children attend private kindergartens, school officially starts at age six, or first grade. Most children continue their studies for another four years in high school.

The overall curriculum includes a firm foundation in English and a second language. The second language studied depends on the student's native tongue. Chinese students learn Mandarin, Malays learn Bahasa Melayu, and Indians study Tamil.

In fifth and seventh grades, students are streamed, or routed, according to their abilities. In high school, students are either placed in express programs that prepare them for standardized British examinations or in less intensive programs. The less intensive programs offer fewer subjects and emphasize core subjects and technical skills. After high school, many students study for their advanced Singapore-Cambridge certificates. After these courses, students attend universities or polytechnics.

Below: **Computer-based lessons are becoming more common in Singaporean schools.**

Left: Singapore Polytechnic offers a wide range of diploma-level programs.

Higher Education

Singapore has three universities, four polytechnics, and many private institutions offering distance-education courses. The National University of Singapore (NUS) has a current enrollment of over twenty thousand students. Nine graduate schools and many research centers offer advanced degrees. Nanyang Technological University (NTU) has an enrollment of twenty thousand students and offers a wide range of engineering-based degrees. Established in 1999, the Singapore Management University (SMU) is working together with the Wharton School of the University of Pennsylvania to develop business courses.

Singapore's four polytechnics educate another sixty thousand Singaporeans. These polytechnics focus on information technology, business, and engineering.

Distance education is an option for working adults who wish to upgrade their skills to advance their careers. Students enroll with Singapore-based representatives of foreign universities, most of which are based in the United States, the United Kingdom, and Australia.

ASSESSMENT BOOKS

Bookstores throughout the country sell plenty of assessment books. These books have many questions and exercises to help students prepare for their examinations.

Above: **Buddhists make offerings and pray for blessings at a temple in Singapore.**

Religion

Singapore's constitution guarantees freedom of worship. The only restriction the government imposes on religious worship is that it does not threaten the well-being of the nation.

About 85 percent of Singaporean citizens follow some form of religion. About 51 percent of the population is Buddhist. Buddhists in Singapore often incorporate elements of Taoism and Confucianism. They honor wise men such as Buddha and Confucius, seek harmony with nature, worship ancestors, and aim to lead simple lives that will lead to truth and enlightenment.

About 15 percent of the resident population, including Malays and a small portion of the Indian community, is Muslim. Muslims worship *Allah* (AH-lah), as revealed by the Prophet Muhammad. Their faith requires that they pray five times a day, fast for one month each year, help the poor, and go on a pilgrimage, or *haj* (HAHJ), to Mecca at least once in their lives.

Approximately 15 percent of Singaporeans are Christians. About one-third of this group is Roman Catholic. The remaining Christian denominations are Anglican, Presbyterian, Lutheran, Methodist, Baptist, and Pentecostal.

HINDU DEITIES

Hindus worship thousands of gods and goddesses, but the three most important are Brahma, the god of creation; Vishnu, the preserver of the universe; and Siva, who is both destroyer and creator of the universe.

Hindus make up 3.3 percent of the population, and almost all worshipers are Indian. Hinduism is based on the *Vedas*, a collection of sacred ancient scriptures. The goal of the faith is to achieve release from reincarnation by performing good deeds and living in peace and harmony with one's fellow men and women.

Celebrating Diversity

Singapore honors and celebrates its multireligious identity with national holidays for each ethnic group. Christmas and Good Friday, representing the birth and death of Christ, are Christian holidays. Chinese New Year celebrates the beginning of the Chinese lunar year, and *Vesak* (VAY-sahk) Day commemorates the birth of Buddha. Muslims have *Hari Raya Puasa* (HAH-ree RYE-ah PWAH-sah), a celebration after a month of fasting, and *Hari Raya Haji* (HAH-ree RYE-ah HAHJ-jee), which honors the pilgrimage to Mecca. *Deepavali* (dee-PAHV-ah-lee) is celebrated by all Indians as a festival of good conquering evil.

Muslims and Hindus have their own councils that act as advisors to the government on religious issues that affect their communities. These councils also maintain the Muslim mosques and Hindu temples in the country.

WAYANG PERFORMANCES
Chinese *wayang* (WHY-yang), or street opera performances (*above*), are a popular form of entertainment that traces its roots back to Singapore's earliest Chinese immigrants.
(A Closer Look, page 70)

JOINING THE CELEBRATIONS

Many of Singapore's ethnic holidays have festivities that include people of all religions and ethnic groups. For example, the *Chingay* (CHIN-gay) street parade held at the end of Chinese New Year also features Malay and Indian performers.

Left: Hindu temples in Singapore feature ornate statues of their goddesses and gods.

Language and Literature

Singapore has four official languages: English, Mandarin (Chinese), Malay, and Tamil (Indian). Malay is the country's national language. While most Singaporeans speak English or Mandarin, English is the most commonly spoken language when at work.

The earliest settlers in Singapore spoke Malay, the language of the region. English took over as the language of trade and business after Singapore became a British colony. Malay, however, remained the most common form of communication between the ethnic groups until the 1960s. After that time, English slowly became the dominant language among the groups because parents felt their children needed to know English to succeed.

The first immigrants from China spoke many Chinese dialects. Their children learned English and Mandarin in school, but continued to speak their native dialects at home. Today, most Chinese Singaporeans are fluent in both Mandarin and English. About two percent of this group still speaks a dialect at home.

Left: Multilingual signs help accommodate the multiethnic population of Singapore.

28

Literary Heritage

Each ethnic group in Singapore has a rich literary heritage from the country of its origin. The Indians have the *Ramayana*; the Malays have oral traditions and the *Malay Annals;* and the Chinese have folk legends and the teachings of Confucius. Singaporeans, however, prefer to concentrate on the literature they have created as a nation since 1965.

Many writers of short stories, plays, and poetry have emerged in the young nation. They tend to write about their experiences in an Asian nation in a changing world. Catherine Lim Poh Imm (1942–) is known internationally for her novels and short stories. She also is an outspoken advocate of women's and human rights. Goh Poh Seng (1936–) and Edwin Thumboo (1933–) are well-known poets.

Playwright Kuo Pao Kun (1939–) is known throughout Asia for his allegorical plays that have universal appeal because they address issues of family, urbanization, and Asia as seen through Asian eyes. Playwright Robert Yeo Cheng Chuan (1940–) has published many prize-winning works.

Above: Reading a newspaper is just one way Singaporeans keep themselves occupied while riding the Mass Rapid Transit (MRT).

Below: Catherine Lim Poh Imm is one of the most widely known authors in Singapore.

Arts

Singapore is fast becoming a regional hub for the performing arts. Theater groups such as The Necessary Stage offer sophisticated local entertainment, while music festivals feature both classical and contemporary groups.

The National Arts Council (NAC) encourages all forms of local and international art. The council's activities include sponsoring writing and music competitions. The council also organizes the annual month-long Singapore Arts Festival. This event includes over three hundred performances by more than one hundred local and international groups. Cultural awards and government assistance programs encourage young artists. A massive new performing arts center, called the Esplanade, is being built to accommodate Singapore's blossoming arts scene.

In the last ten years, interest in the arts has grown rapidly. New experimental groups are developing throughout the country, and Singapore is an ideal place for people interested in creative or unusual forms of theater and visual art.

Below: The Singapore Art Museum was formerly a high school for boys founded by Christian missionaries.

Visual Arts

The Nanyang Academy of Fine Arts (NAFA) was established in 1938 and LaSalle-SIA College of the Arts in 1984. Both institutions offer diplomas and degrees in the arts, and many local talents have received their training at these schools.

The Singapore Art Museum features contemporary Southeast Asian art, especially the works of Singaporean artists. The museum also hosts major international exhibitions. For example, the works of Leonardo da Vinci were exhibited in 1998.

Since the 1960s, artists have focused on multicultural and international styles with some Asian or Singaporean influence. Among the works are the watercolors of Ong Kim Seng (1945–) and sculptures by Ng Eng Teng (1934–).

Singapore's visual arts community organizes cultural exchanges and exhibitions to showcase local works overseas. In 1995, the NAC organized one of its biggest overseas exhibitions, which toured seven cities in China. Singapore also hosts several major visual arts events such as the annual United Overseas Bank (UOB) Painting of the Year Competition, which helps identify new talent, and the biennial Singapore Art Competition.

Above: **This work by Taiwanese sculptor Ju Ming is part of his** *The Living World* **series of sculptures. The sculpture was bought by the Singapore History Museum in 1987 and is located outside the museum.**

ART PIONEER

Georgette Chen came to Singapore in 1954 and taught art at NAFA for twenty-six years. She developed as an artist in Paris and exhibited her works in Paris, Shanghai, and New York.

Architecture

Although most of Singapore's cityscape is dominated by skyscrapers and shopping malls, traditional forms of architecture can still be found. Conservation efforts have saved many old buildings, such as pre-World War II shophouses, from being torn down. The National Heritage Board tries to preserve these old buildings without losing their cultural significance. Some architects try to design buildings that feature elements of colonial and Asian architecture.

Theater and Dance

Singapore is finding its artistic voice in the performing arts. Chinese, Malay, Tamil, and English theater groups perform plays that express national and Asian concerns and the universal themes of life, love, and death. Kuo Pao Kun, who runs the Chinese-language group Practice Theatre Ensemble, is one of Singapore's most revered playwrights. Director Ong Keng Sen has staged a multicultural performance of *King Lear*, using English dialogue and Asian dance forms. Malay theater groups,

Above: **Many old shophouses have been refurbished and are now used as offices, restaurants, and bars.**

Below: **The intricate carvings on some old shophouses have been restored to their former glory.**

such as Teater Kami, and Indian groups, including Agni Koothu, stage plays that reflect the changing concerns of Singapore's Malay and Indian communities.

The Singapore Dance Theatre was established in 1988 and performs ballet, classical, and modern dance. The signature work of the company is a repertoire choreographed by Goh Choo San (1948–1987), which he had originally done for the Washington Ballet in the United States.

Music

The Singapore Symphony Orchestra (SSO) performs about one hundred times a year, and the Singapore Chinese Orchestra gives about twenty performances annually. SSO founder Choo Hoey and Lim Yau are well-known conductors. Internationally known Singapore artists, such as violinist Siow Lee Chin and pianist Seow Yit Kin, have performed with the SSO.

Listening to music, whether on the radio, at concerts, or on MTV, is a popular pastime in Singapore. Annual musical events, such as the Singapore International Jazz Festival, attract a large local and overseas following.

ROOM TO MOVE
Theaters abound in Singapore, and about half a million people attend performances yearly. The Victoria Theater has been an established performance arena for many years, while The Substation is a venue for experimental theater and original art.

Below: Ballet is becoming a popular activity among young Singaporeans. It is even taught in some schools.

Leisure and Festivals

Out and About

Singaporeans enjoy good food, and almost every leisure activity involves a meal. Eating out at a restaurant or food court gives friends and family a chance to meet and exchange the latest news. Often on Sundays, the entire family will have breakfast at a coffee shop or fast-food restaurant and then buy the weekly groceries.

Many Singaporeans enjoy day-long excursions to Malaysia, which is just a short drive away. Although Malaysia is close, the country is quite different from Singapore. It has bustling urban centers as well as rural resorts that offer Singaporeans a sense of space.

From flower arranging to line-dancing classes, community clubs around the island organize many activities. Many people also enjoy outdoor sports, such as cycling, jogging, and golf.

Teenagers like to hang out with their friends at shopping malls. Cyber cafés that allow customers to play multiplayer computer games are another popular choice. Teenagers also enjoy

Below: **Most Singaporeans enjoy dining out and visiting with friends and family.**

34

music and listen to the latest Eastern and Western musical styles. Like their parents, teenagers often meet for meals in restaurants or food courts.

At Home

At home, enjoyable activities may include listening to the radio, watching television, playing computer games, and surfing the Internet. More than half of all Singaporean homes are connected to the Internet. In fact, so many Singaporeans access the Internet on Sundays it is sometimes difficult to retrieve E-mail.

Singaporeans are enthusiastic collectors and great believers in games of chance. Telephone cards, dolls, and stamps are just some examples of popular collectors items. The weekly lottery is also supported by Singaporeans who hope to strike it rich. For example, if the grocery bill contains the same sequence of numbers as their postal code, they might bet this number in the "4-digit" weekly lottery.

SINGAPORE ONLINE

Computers are part of everyday life in Singapore, as the country seeks to become an IT-savvy "Intelligent Island." The country is moving swiftly toward developing a global, knowledge-based economy.
(*A Closer Look, page 62*)

Left: Soccer is one of the most popular sports in Singapore.

Above: Weightlifter Tan Howe Liang has won Singapore's only Olympic medal so far.

Sports

Soccer and track and field are among the favorite student sports in Singapore. Mostly boys play soccer, but more than 8,500 boys and girls participate in track and field events all over the island. The Singapore Sports Council's "Sports for Life" program promotes sports as a healthy way of life. The program encourages Singaporeans to participate in nationwide events, such as walkathons, swimming competitions, and fitness promotions. Most housing estates have comprehensive public sports facilities that include swimming pools, tennis courts, and stadiums.

Spectator Sports

Soccer is a popular spectator sport in Singapore. Singapore's professional league, the S-League, has eight teams that compete against one another in stadiums throughout the country. The national soccer team participates in the Southeast Asian (SEA) Games and the World Cup championship qualifying matches.

Horse racing is another popular spectator sport in Singapore. Horse races are held in Singapore or Malaysia every weekend. Even when the races are held in Malaysia, many fans go to the track in Singapore to watch the horses on big-screen televisions.

Dragon boat racing is an unusual spectator sport along the Singapore River. Every June, rowing teams from all over the world race against one another in brightly decorated boats. The bow of each boat resembles the head of a dragon.

International Competitions

Singapore's most successful competitive sport is swimming. In 1982, Ang Peng Siong held the world record for the 50-meter freestyle. In the 1990s, Ang Peng Siong and Joscelin Yeo broke swimming records in the SEA Games, and Neo Chwee Kok won four gold medals in the Asian Games.

Singaporean athletes also excel in Ping-Pong, or table tennis, and bowling at competitions such as the Asian Games and SEA Games. One of Singapore's greatest athletes was Wong Peng Soon. He won four All England Badminton championships and was the best singles' player in the world in the early 1950s. So far, weightlifter Tan Howe Liang has won Singapore's only Olympic medal, winning the silver at the 1960 Rome Olympics.

AERIAL BALLET

Sepak takraw (seh-PAHK TAHK-raw) is a sport unique to Southeast Asia. The game is similar to volleyball, except that players use only their feet. The object of the game is to keep the rattan, or cane ball, in the air by kicking it over a high net. A team loses a point each time it allows the ball to touch the ground.

Below: Singapore's water polo team has won eighteen consecutive gold medals in the biennial Southeast Asian Games.

Ethnic Festivals

Singapore celebrates many ethnic festivals throughout the year, honoring the country's multicultural population. Chinese New Year, held in January or February, is the most widely celebrated holiday of the year since three-fourths of the resident population are Chinese. Most shops and offices close for at least the first two days of the Chinese New Year period.

On the eve of the holiday, most Chinese celebrate with a traditional family reunion dinner. The next two days are spent visiting family and friends to wish them *gong xi fa chai* (GOHNG see FAH chie), or an auspicious new year. Unmarried children receive *hong bao* (HUNG bough), a small red envelope that contains money. Visiting and feasting continue for fifteen days.

Singapore's Indian community celebrates three main Hindu festivals — Deepavali, *Thimithi* (TIH-mih-tee), and *Thaipusam* (TIE-poo-sahm). Deepavali, the Festival of Lights, celebrates the victory of good over evil. Families visit Hindu temples to pray to their goddesses and gods, then feast together.

Above: **Singaporeans preparing for Chinese New Year festivities shop for decorations in Chinatown.**

Hindus believe the souls of departed relatives come down to Earth during this time. Families light tiny earthen oil lamps in the home to guide these souls as they return to the next world.

Thimithi is a fire-walking ceremony in which devotees walk on hot coals. During the Thaipusam festival, followers carry elaborate wooden or metal headdresses known as *kavadis* (KAH-vah-dees). Both festivals are celebrated to ask for forgiveness or as a sign of thanksgiving. Devotees must pray and fast for several months before participating in either of these festivals.

Malays and other Muslims in Singapore celebrate important dates in Islam. Hari Raya Puasa celebrates the end of *Ramadan* (RAH-mah-dahn), the Muslim month of fasting. Hari Raya Haji celebrates the pilgrimage to Mecca. Muslims slaughter a lamb for this celebration, prepare special dishes, and share their food with the poor. Muslims often invite non-Muslim friends to their homes to join the celebrations.

PROTECTION AND PROSPERITY

Lion and dragon dances are often performed in Singapore. Lions are believed to ward off evil and bring good luck. Dragons represent strength and power.

Left: A devotee carries a kavadi during the Thaipusam festival. The kavadi bears offerings of fruits, flowers, and milk.

Food

Singaporean food is as exotic and varied as its peoples. Spicy Chinese cuisine, tantalizing curries, and wonderful breads come from its rich Chinese, Malay, and Indian heritage. Eating styles are as varied as the cuisine. Although knives and forks are always available, Chinese food is usually eaten with chopsticks, while Malay and Indian diners use a fork and spoon and sometimes their right hand.

Malay, Chinese, and Indian Favorites

Chinese food in Singapore may be Cantonese, which has a fresh delicate flavor, such as stir-fried beef in oyster sauce or steamed fish with ginger; or Teochew, which offers slightly sour sauces and preserved vegetables. Spicy Szechuan dishes, Peking duck, and chicken rice from Hainan are also popular, as are Hokkien soups and rich sauces, Hainanese steamed chicken in lotus leaves, and Hakka fried shrimp.

A popular form of Singaporean Chinese food is a mix of Malay and Chinese cuisine. The dishes can be hot and spicy or

EATING OUT

Singapore is famous for its offerings of delicious international cuisine and exotic fruits, including the durian (*above*).
(*A Closer Look, page 44*)

Left: *Char kway teow* (CHAH kway tee-ow), or fried flat noodles, is a favorite Singaporean dish.

flavored with a delicate blend of coconut milk and tangy herbs. Chili crab, for example, has a thick, rich sauce made with tiny, fiery chilis and ginger, while noodle, or *mee* (ME), soup is a mild broth containing shrimp, fish balls, and green vegetables. Noodle dishes can be stir-fried or served with or without soup.

Many Malay dishes are made with coconut milk, chilis, and other spices. Muslims do not eat pork, but a typical *nasi padang* (NAH-see PAH-dahng), or rice buffet, offers chicken, shrimp, and beef curries; fried fish; and vegetables.

A typical South Indian meal has vegetable, chickpea, and lentil dishes served with yogurt, chutney, and rice. North Indian *vindaloo* (VIN-dah-loo) is a fiery hot tomato and chicken or lamb stew, best eaten with rice and *raita* (rye-EE-tah), which is yogurt mixed with cucumbers and herbs.

Desserts tend to be bland, perhaps because the meals are rich and spicy. Desserts are often layered sponge cakes or jell-O-like dishes or puddings. Fresh fruit is popular, especially papaya, oranges, mangoes, and watermelons.

A CLOSER LOOK AT SINGAPORE

Singapore is a nation of contrasts. Mobile phone-carrying Singaporeans still enjoy old-fashioned Chinese opera and see omens in every aspect of life. They treasure the heritage of their ancestors, but they are proud of what they have accomplished as a modern nation.

The island has many highways and high-rise buildings, but beautiful parks are everywhere, and lush greenery lines most roadsides. Although Singapore has been an independent nation only since 1965, the country has a rich cultural history. Malay, Chinese, Indian, and British cultures have had a huge impact

Opposite: **Colorful outdoor markets attract many people in Singapore and are often located near large shopping centers.**

on its development. The success of this tiny country is largely due to the drive of Lee Kuan Yew, who served as prime minister from 1959 to 1990.

Singaporeans are ambitious and determined to make their nation a regional base for business, technology, and the arts. They have a well-developed economy, an efficient infrastructure, and a state-of-the-art defense force. Most of all, they have created a prosperous, beautiful, safe, and welcoming country for visitors and citizens.

Above: **Visitors to the Qian Hu Fish Farm can see over five hundred species of ornamental fish from around the world.**

Eating Out

Eating out is a popular pastime in Singapore. With so many street stalls, food courts, and restaurants offering such a wide variety of choices, it is no surprise that Singapore is a delightful place for food lovers.

It is a common sight to see friends and families gathered around a table, enjoying a delicious meal at one of Singapore's numerous eating places. For many Singaporeans, eating out or buying a carry-out meal from a restaurant is usually the most practical way to fit a meal into their busy schedules. After a long day at the office, many Singaporeans simply do not have the time or the energy to cook a meal at home.

The cheapest, and some would say the most delicious, meals can be enjoyed at coffee shops and hawker centers. Coffee shops are usually located on the ground floors of apartment buildings in housing estates. They are small and usually have less than ten

Below: Satay **(SAH-tay) is a Malay delicacy made by skewering small pieces of meat and cooking them over an open flame.**

Left: Spicy delicacies such as fish head curry (*center, top*) and chili crab (*bottom, left*) are popular dishes among locals and tourists.

stalls selling mostly local food. Hawker centers are larger and have several dozen stalls that sell a wider variety of Asian fare. These structures are located either in housing estates or popular spots such as the beach along the East Coast.

Food courts are found in shopping malls. Although the food there is slightly more expensive than at hawker centers, food courts offer a wider choice of food. It is not unusual for Korean, Italian, and Japanese foods to be sold alongside local dishes. Children and teenagers enjoy fast-food restaurants, which can be found almost everywhere in Singapore.

Cafés such as Starbucks and Coffee Club have become increasingly popular in recent years, especially among young working adults. These cafes serve Western foods, such as sandwiches and pasta. Eating at these places can be relatively expensive — a cup of coffee alone can cost as much as a meal in a food court!

Singapore has many restaurants to cater to every taste and budget. Relatively inexpensive restaurants are popular choices with families and large groups of friends. At the other end of the scale, a meal at more exclusive restaurants, such as The Compass Rose, can easily cost a few hundred dollars.

Above: A *roti prata* (ROH-tee PRAH-tah) seller cooks this Indian delicacy on a large, circular pan. Roti prata is a traditional Indian pancake made from flour. It is usually served with curry and can be cooked plain or with an egg or onion filling.

Housing for the People

Singapore has successfully housed virtually all of its citizens through an intensive building program headed by the Housing and Development Board (HDB). Today, about 86 percent of all Singaporeans live in relatively low-cost, high-rise apartments.

The HDB initiative, however, was much more than a housing project. The program was an impressive and successful feat of both integration and national self-esteem. In the late 1950s, the primary objective of the HDB was to provide inexpensive rental apartments. The priority was to solve the problems of overcrowding and dismal living conditions.

As time went by, the HDB began to deal with the communal nature of the country. Racial quotas were established block by block and community by community. The people of Chinatown and overcrowded villages were dispersed throughout the island in apartments that reflected the ethnic makeup of the country. In other words, each building and each community was about

Below: **This scene from Chinatown in the 1950s shows the crowded living conditions many Singaporeans had to endure at the time.**

Above: **Eighty-six percent of Singapore's population lives in high-rise public housing projects.**

three-quarters Chinese and one-quarter Malay and Indian. The HDB hoped that, by breaking up the ethnic concentrations of the past and forcing one group to live next to another in the housing estates, the barriers among the ethnic groups would be torn down. The mixing of groups ensured that politicians could not appeal to any one particular ethnic group to get elected to Parliament, effectively eliminating ethnic politics.

In the mid-1960s, the emphasis shifted from providing rental apartments to selling them to the people. Home ownership was intended as a way to convince people they had a stake in the country. The government also hoped that home ownership would lead to a sense of pride in the community.

The program has been a great success. Today, the housing estates are vibrant, multiethnic towns. Each estate has a wide range of facilities, including clinics and schools. Each town is divided into neighborhoods of about twenty-four thousand people, and each neighborhood is subdivided into precincts of two thousand to three thousand people.

Immigrants: Then and Now

Although Singapore is a Southeast Asian country, many of its people originally came from China, India, and the Malay archipelago. In the new millennium, Singapore is once again opening its doors to people from beyond its shores.

Many of the immigrants who came to Singapore during its early years were Peranakans. Their knowledge of the region and their local ties provided an important commercial link between Singapore and the Malay archipelago. Later, Chinese and Indian laborers provided the economy with low-cost, hardworking labor that helped fuel its growth. The Straits Chinese, Malays, and Indians who stayed and settled in the country became the colony's first true Singaporeans.

Immigrant Labor

Today, a new wave of immigration is taking place. Singapore's success is drawing new immigrants from all over the world. Singapore has a population of about four million people, only 75 percent of whom are citizens. Since 1990, the percentage of people on the island who are not Singaporean has risen from 10 percent to 25 percent.

By the 1980s, as a result of falling birthrates, Singapore's population was too small to support its economy. Foreign workers were brought in to work in factories, construct new buildings, and serve as maids. By the end of the twentieth century, Singapore had more than 300,000 immigrant workers.

Professional Labor

In the 1990s, further economic growth required not only unskilled labor, but skilled, educated workers as well. Singapore needed people skilled in professions such as finance and information technology. Therefore, Singaporean businesses began recruiting immigrants from all over the world. The number of noncitizen residents tripled from about 100,000 to around 300,000. The number of immigrant semiskilled workers rose to about 700,000. Once again, Singapore is attracting people looking for a better life for themselves and their families.

Above: Singapore's early immigrants settled in small villages like this one. Rapid urbanization has virtually eliminated these small communities.

Opposite: Many Singaporeans today can trace their roots to China, India, or the Malaysian Peninsula.

49

The Japanese Occupation

The Japanese occupation of Singapore for three-and-a-half years during World War II was a dramatic turning point in Singapore's history. At that time, no one in British Malaya thought Britain could be defeated. The Japanese, however, had other ideas, and in just ten short weeks, the Japanese army conquered Singapore.

All the Westerners and many local residents who had worked in the civil service prior to the Japanese occupation were imprisoned. The Japanese demanded the absolute loyalty of the people. Locals were often punished for committing even the

Below: **The loss of Singapore to Japanese forces during World War II was a major blow to British standing in the Straits Settlements. A multimedia diorama of the British surrender is recreated here in the "Images of Singapore" exhibit on Sentosa Island.**

slightest offense, such as not bowing to an officer. Accused criminals were beheaded in public. Thousands of Chinese were rounded up for being anti-Japanese or communist. They were tortured and even executed if the Japanese suspected them of committing acts of treason. Many were executed simply because they were Chinese.

The Japanese occupation also shattered Singapore's booming economy. The Chinese, who were an essential element of the retail and distribution system, were uncooperative because the

Japanese treated them badly. Inexperienced Japanese military personnel and civilians took over the running of the government and the economy.

Trade was disrupted because the Japanese navy did not have enough ships and was spread too thinly to control the sea lanes. Most of Singapore's food had been imported and paid for by the profits from trade. Now the small volume of trade meant that very little food could be bought. The Japanese made matters worse by printing large amounts of paper money. The money was called "banana money" because of the pictures of bananas on the bills. Soon, the banana money was almost worthless. For example, 1 pound (450 grams) of sugar had cost S$0.08 before World War II. By the end of the war, the same amount of sugar cost S$120.

Above: **Fort Canning Centre was a British Army barracks during World War II. Today, it hosts the Singapore Dance Theatre and TheatreWorks, two modern performing arts companies.**

Some Singaporeans slipped into the Malayan jungles and formed resistance groups. The most famous of these guerillas was a businessman named Lim Bo Seng.

The British returned to Singapore in September 1945 after the Allies won World War II. Although the people celebrated the return of the British, their feelings toward Britain had changed. The British had not protected them from invasion and occupation, and the people of Singapore had suffered for more than three years. As a result, they began a quest for independence.

Land from the Sea

In 1964, Singapore began a land reclamation program to tackle the problem of its limited land area. At that time, the country's land area totaled 224 square miles (580 square km). By 1999, the total land size was 255 square miles (660 square km). Singapore plans to add another 39 squares miles (100 square km) in the future.

Reclaiming Land

When the government decides to reclaim land from the sea, the Urban Redevelopment Authority (URA) studies the site to decide if the soil and seabed are suitable for construction. Then, it does an environmental impact study to determine if reclaiming works will adversely affect tidal flow and water level or cause excessive buildup of sediment. The URA also tries to minimize damage to the islands's remaining coral reefs. Almost 60 percent of these reefs were destroyed in the earliest reclamation projects.

Below: **These hotels and shopping malls in Marina Center have all been built on reclaimed land.**

The reclamation process begins with piling machines that stabilize the soft clay seabed. These machines press the sand down hard and insert vertical drains to remove excess water in the clay. Then a sand wall is built around the area to be filled, and barges unload sand just outside the walled area. This sand is then pumped through pipes into the area inside the walls until it is above sea level. Sometimes the sand is dumped directly into the walled area. The new land is then compacted by rollers. Plants such as creeping vines, rough grass, and casuarina pines are planted to help stabilize the new shore area. The sand seawall is rebuilt with granite to reinforce the reclaimed area and prevent its return to the sea through erosion and storms.

In 1976, 1,638 acres (663 ha) of land were reclaimed on the eastern coast of the island, but nothing could be built on the land immediately. Reclaimed land needs to settle for one to five years before any structure can be built on it. Changi International Airport, which was built on this site, and the beautiful, flower-lined East Coast Parkway, which takes visitors directly into the city, did not open until 1981.

Above: Reclamation has helped the land area of Singapore grow by more than 10 percent in the last forty years.

THE FIRST LAND RECLAMATION PROJECT

Reclaiming land actually began in Singapore in 1822, when city planners drained a swamp along the Singapore River. Today, that site is known as Raffles Place, the heart of Singapore's commercial district.

Lee Kuan Yew

Lee Kuan Yew is widely acknowledged as the man who led Singapore to nationhood. He was born in 1923 in Singapore to a Straits Chinese family who had lived in the country for several decades. Lee completed his education at Cambridge University in Britain, where he studied law. When Lee returned from Britain in 1950, he had ambitious plans to free Singapore from colonial rule. In 1954, he founded the People's Action Party together with compatriots such as Toh Chin Chye.

Lee bridged many of the gaps between the English-speaking Straits Chinese, who had resided in the area for generations, and the Chinese-speaking immigrants who came to Singapore in the 1930s and 1940s. The latter group was attracted to radical leaders, such as communists, because they had suffered the most from the lack of jobs and housing. Lee understood their hopes had to be

A NARROW ESCAPE

During the Japanese occupation of Singapore in World War II, Lee Kuan Yew was detained by the Japanese and was supposedly going to be sent on a work party. In reality, the Japanese planned to execute him. Lee sensed the danger and asked the guards if he could take some of his belongings from the detention center. They let him go, and he managed to escape.

Left: Lee Kuan Yew talks to young residents at Bukit Ho Swee housing estate in 1965. This former squatter colony had been razed by a fire four years earlier.

met if Singapore was to succeed. More than thirty years later, Singapore had become a bustling metropolis with one of the highest per capita incomes in the world.

Although Lee is greatly respected by most Singaporeans, not everyone has agreed with his methods. Many observers, especially those in the West, believe individual liberties were neglected for the sake of economic progress. Lee and the PAP entered into an informal agreement with the Singaporean people. The population was asked to accept more government control and work hard. In return, the PAP would give them a stable environment and a good standard of living.

Lee served as prime minister from 1959 to 1990, when he stepped down and was replaced by Goh Chok Tong. A new cabinet position, that of senior minister, was created, making it possible for Lee to continue to play an active role in Parliament. Today, Lee continues to influence Singapore's policies and direction. His experience and vision are seen as important resources to Singapore's newer political leaders.

Parks

Singapore has several nature reserves and parks that allow visitors to quietly enjoy nature. In all, Singapore has about 5,782 acres (2,340 ha) of parks and open spaces.

Bukit Timah Nature Reserve is a popular spot for hiking. Narrow footpaths lead up Bukit Timah Hill, and the summit offers a breathtaking view of the island. Sungei Buloh Nature Park is a bird sanctuary and wetland area. About one hundred species of birds, which migrate between countries to the north and south of Singapore, visit the park each year. The Jurong BirdPark and Singapore Zoological Gardens are known not only as popular tourist destinations, but also for their conservation efforts.

Botanic Gardens

Singapore's Botanic Gardens teems with lush tropical plants and is a beautiful spot for picnics, open-air concerts, and jogging. The park is a 128-acre (52-ha) paradise right in the middle of the city. Birds, squirrels, and lizards can be seen along nature trails.

Below: The Jurong BirdPark has many species of birds, such as these flamingos. It is a popular spot for everyone who loves nature.

The park was established in 1859 as a pleasure park. Later, the park became a botanical and experimental garden for spices, rubber trees, and orchids. Today, the park also acts as an educational center. Students can learn about the plants by reading plaques and viewing exhibits at the visitor's center.

Orchids have always grown well in tropical Singapore, and the Botanic Gardens has twenty thousand orchid plants on display. By the 1930s, Singapore was producing many hybrid orchids, which are a cross of two different orchid species. Today, orchids are a multimillion-dollar export business.

High-Tech Farms

Although most of Singapore's food is imported, a few small farms grow vegetables and breed poultry. Every farm uses sophisticated computerized equipment to research and develop the products it produces.

Vegetables, especially lettuce and herbs, are grown in pesticide-free greenhouses. These greenhouses often use hydroponics, a method of growing plants without the use of soil. Fish farms raise grouper, sea bass, snapper, and shrimp for local consumption and export. Ornamental fish, such as dragon fish, are also raised for export. Other farms breed crocodiles and birds.

Below: Orchids from Singapore are exported all over the world.

Raffles Outwits the Dutch

Although Singapore was an important trading center in the seventeenth century, very few people lived on the island when Sir Thomas Stamford Raffles arrived in 1819. Raffles was determined to establish a center for British trade on the Strait of Malacca. The British already controlled Penang in the northern part of the Malay peninsula. They also had some bases in what is now Indonesia but did not control the area in between. Singapore was perfect because it was in the middle of the trade routes between the Moluccas and China to the east and India and Britain to the west. Traders would stop there to buy fuel and supplies.

Singapore, however, belonged to the Dutch at the time, and the Malay sultan was a Dutch representative. Raffles also did not have permission from his employers, the East India Company, to invade Dutch lands. However, he knew the base would be important to British interests in the region.

Raffles' first action was to "legalize" British rule over the island. Sultan Abdul Rahman, who had been appointed by the Dutch in 1818, had an older brother named Hussein who also claimed the Johor throne. Raffles made a deal with the territorial chief, or *temenggong* (tuh-MUNG-gohng), to appoint the brother as the sultan of Singapore. Sultan Hussein then signed a treaty with Raffles, making Singapore a British possession. This agreement was not recognized by the Malay royalty, but Singapore grew so rapidly under British control that Malay interests were of little importance once the British had the "official" document. The Dutch and British were angry with Raffles. Raffles, however, ignored their protests. Traders from all over Southeast Asia flocked to Singapore. By 1821, the port was so prosperous that the British did not want to return the island to the Dutch.

Negotiations led to the Anglo-Dutch Treaty of 1824, which divided present-day Malaysia and Indonesia into British and Dutch spheres of influence, respectively. The Malay peoples were divided by an arbitrary line through the Strait of Malacca. The British and Dutch now controlled trade, and the indigenous traders were no longer powerful.

Above: **Sir Thomas Stamford Raffles risked sparking a war with the Dutch when he founded Singapore in 1819.**

Opposite: **Soon after founding Singapore, Raffles left the colony and did not return until 1822. Most of the early development of Singapore was planned by his subordinate, William Farquhar.**

Ready to Mobilize

All male citizens in Singapore are required to serve in the Singapore Armed Forces (SAF). The men are called up right after high school. No physically fit male is exempt from National Service (NS), and the law requires that all men serve NS for either two or two-and-a-half years. When their NS stint is over, the men can still be called back to their units for up to forty days a year for training until they reach the age of forty. Officers must serve part-time until they are fifty years old. Singaporean reserve troops are expected to keep fit all year long to stay ready for combat at all times. Among other things, they must be able to run 1.5 miles (2.4 km) in less than 12 minutes. Their fitness is tested when they rejoin their units each year. About 20,000 career soldiers and 55,000 National Servicemen serve in the army, navy, and air force. In addition, 225,000 trained reservists are ready to serve within a few hours' notice.

Below: **National Service builds maturity, self-confidence, and strength.**

Then and Now

When the British armed forces began to withdraw from Singapore in 1967, the country was left with only two infantry battalions, no aircraft, and a few patrol boats. Today, the SAF is one of the best-equipped armed forces in the region. Troops use sophisticated simulators that can create battle scenarios. For example, electronic indoor shooting ranges use projection screens and sound effects to simulate the sights and sounds of battle. Each soldier's hits are recorded and displayed after each "battle."

The SAF sends medical detachments and other support personnel to crisis areas around the world, such as East Timor in 1999. Singaporean forces have also participated in several United Nations (U.N.) peacekeeping efforts. The SAF also trains with the armed forces of other countries, such as the United States.

The growth of the SAF has spurred the growth of companies that specialize in weapons and technology. Singapore Technologies has subsidiaries that build everything from weapons to train regulation systems.

Above: **These officer cadets from the Republic of Singapore Navy (RSN) are rehearsing for an upcoming parade.**

WEAPONS PRODUCTION

Chartered Industries, a subsidiary of Singapore Technologies, was formed in 1967 to manufacture M16 rifles and ammunition under license. Today, the company manufactures a wide range of locally designed weapons, from the SAR21 assault rifle to howitzers and even light tanks.

Singapore Online

Singaporeans are obsessed with being "in the know." They are big fans of the Internet, mobile phones, and any twenty-first century innovation that keeps them well-informed. Singapore has the highest rate of Internet users in Asia — 46 percent of all citizens over the age of fifteen go online every month, while 53 percent of all households are connected to the Internet.

The entire country seems to be run by computer technology. Traffic is regulated by a sophisticated road-pricing system. Every car has an electronic device into which the driver must insert a "cash card." An overhead gantry automatically deducts payment when the vehicle enters a restricted area. Restricted areas include the shopping and business districts.

Cash cards can be used for many transactions, including buying groceries, checking out library books, and having a document photocopied. Almost every building has an automated teller machine (ATM). Public buses have machines that deduct fees from a fare card, which stores money in an electronic format.

Left: This Electronic Road Pricing (ERP) gantry is near Orchard Road. ERP was introduced to curb traffic congestion in the city center.

Paying bills by automatic deduction from a bank account is greatly encouraged. Some organizations even charge extra if bills are paid by check. Singapore plans to become a "cashless society," meaning that all payments will be made electronically.

Above: **Sophisticated computer systems help keep track of the location of MRT trains.**

In Singapore, people who do not know how to use computers usually have a difficult time because so many transactions depend on computer skills. For example, most students do their homework on computers or even submit papers and are graded by E-mail. Many people even file their taxes through the Internet.

Science Hub

Singapore is moving swiftly from a manufacturing- and services-based economy to a global, knowledge-based economy. The country has its own Silicon Valley, called the Science Hub. New and innovative products are created here, and scientists study the latest forms of technology.

"Technopreneurship 21" is a national initiative to develop sophisticated technological devices, support research, and create an environment for the growth of technological expertise.

The Straits Chinese

At the time of the country's independence, Singapore's Straits Chinese community consisted of two groups — the Peranakans and the Straits Chinese who arrived in Singapore in the nineteenth century.

The Peranakans were early Chinese traders and businessmen who married local Malay women. They adopted some aspects of the Malay culture while retaining many Chinese customs, such as the worship of ancestors. A Peranakan man was called *baba* (BAH-bah), and a Peranakan woman was called *nonya* (NYOH-nyah). Babas kept their long Chinese pigtails and pajama-like clothes well into the twentieth century. Nonyas wore Malay clothes, such as a sarong, with a long-sleeved tunic called a *kebaya* (kuh-BYE-yah).

A second, larger wave of Chinese emigrated to Malaya in the nineteenth century. These people became known as the Straits Chinese because they lived in the three British settlements on the Strait of Malacca — Singapore, Malacca, and Penang. They spoke Malay and Chinese but did not adopt Malay culture.

Below: **The Emerald Hill area in central Singapore has a series of about 150 historical Peranakan homes, such as the one pictured here, that were constructed between 1918 and 1930.**

Left: Traditional Peranakan weddings are grand events. The bridal couple wears ornate costumes, and the wedding festivities last for twelve days!

The Peranakans and the Straits Chinese were English-speaking businesspeople who were familiar with regional trade patterns and local business customs. Many moved to Singapore when it became the region's commercial center. They formed close economic ties with the British and adopted many Western customs.

These two groups considered themselves British citizens. They did not mix easily with the Chinese immigrants who came to Singapore in the twentieth century. Despite their differences with the immigrants, the groups sought representation in the British colonial government and fought for a better standard of life for the immigrants. They played an important part in improving Chinese education, ending opium smoking, and improving the status of Chinese women. Many Straits Chinese and Peranakans later became leaders of independent Singapore.

The Peranakans gradually became part of the greater Straits Chinese community. However, they have a special place in Singapore as ethnic Chinese with ancestral roots in Malaya.

EARLY PERANAKAN COMMUNITIES

The children of the initial Peranakan unions did not marry Malays. They married other Peranakans or Chinese, creating a Chinese community with a Malay flavor. When the British came to the area in the nineteenth century, the Peranakans had formed well-established, urban communities.

Tourism

Tourism is one of the cornerstones of the Singaporean economy. In 1999, Singapore earned U.S. $5.8 billion from tourism, and almost 7.7 million tourists visited the island in 2000. This figure set a new record for the number of tourist arrivals in Singapore, beating the previous record of 7.3 million tourists set in 1996. The Singapore Tourism Board (STB) hopes that by 2005, Singapore will attract 10 million tourists each year.

Singapore has spent large sums of money developing its tourism industry and infrastructure. The Singapore Zoological Gardens is just one example of the country's first-class tourist attractions. The 69-acre (28-ha) zoo has 216 species of animals. In addition, it is an "open concept" zoo, which means that the animals are not kept in cages. Instead, they live in enclosures that simulate their natural habitat and are separated from zoo visitors by moats. One offshoot of developing such tourist attractions is that Singaporeans also get to enjoy the facilities.

LARGEST SOURCE OF VISITORS
Indonesia accounted for the biggest slice of Singapore's tourism pie in 2000. Just over 17 percent of the total number of visitors to Singapore came from Indonesia.

Below: The Jurong BirdPark, which opened in 1971, has more than six hundred species of birds.

Tourism 21

The STB has unveiled a plan known as "Tourism 21," to keep the country's tourism industry competitive in the future. Tourism 21 will expand the role Singapore plays in regional tourism. In addition to selling Singapore as a tourist destination, the STB will also market Singapore as a tourism business center and regional tourism hub.

Marketing Singapore as a tourism business center means that the STB will try to encourage tourism-related companies to invest in Singapore. For example, the STB helped tourism-related retail outlets such as Borders bookstore and HMV music store set up shops in Singapore.

Positioning Singapore as a regional tourism hub means that the STB will work with neighboring countries to promote regional tourist destinations. For example, Singapore and Indonesia signed a Tourism Cooperation Package in 2000. The program will promote both countries as complimentary tourist destinations, whereby tourists can visit Singapore and use its tourist facilities to plan trips to neighboring Indonesian islands, such as Bintan and Bali.

Above: **Sentosa Island received 3.3 million visitors in 1999.**

NIGHT SAFARI

The Singapore Zoological Gardens also has a 99-acre (40-ha) Night Safari that is home to over one hundred species of nocturnal animals.

Traditional Beliefs

Many Chinese Singaporeans believe that good and bad luck are inherent in almost every object and deed. For instance, the number eight is considered lucky because the Chinese term for it sounds like *fa* (FAH), which means "prosperity" in Chinese. Double-digit numbers are believed to be a double blessing. Red is a lucky color, and white is associated with death. Dreams and even the moles on a person's face have special meanings, too.

The Chinese calendar contains a cycle of twelve lunar years. Each year is represented by an animal that has good and bad traits. Many Chinese believe a person will have similar traits to the animal that represents his or her year of birth. For instance, many believe girls born in the year of the dragon will grow up to be fierce, and boys will become strong and powerful men.

Many beliefs are associated with *feng shui* (FUNG shway), or geomancy. Feng shui is based on the idea that all things in nature contain yin, or darkness, and yang, or light. The balance of the

THE LUNAR CALENDAR

The Chinese calendar has twelve-year cycles, and an animal represents each year. The animals, in order of appearance, are the rat, bull, tiger, rabbit, dragon, snake, horse, goat, monkey, rooster, dog, and pig.

Below: A geomancer uses a mix of Chinese and Western instruments to determine the flow of energy in a shopping mall.

two forces leads to *chi* (CHEE), or energy. Feng shui beliefs are still practiced in many countries. People who live and work in places that have a good flow of chi are energetic, enterprising, and successful. Misfortunes, such as ill health, bankruptcy, and divorce, are believed to result from bad chi.

Geomancers are often consulted when a building is erected or an apartment chosen because the flow of chi through a room or around a building can be affected by furniture placement or the angle of a wall. For instance, curved office buildings attract prosperity, while straight edges drive it away. A mirror is believed to deflect bad spirits, but too many mirrors will trap them.

A well-known example is how the Hyatt Hotel changed its fortunes in the 1980s. When the hotel first opened, business was poor, so a geomancer was consulted. He noted that the payment desk was very close to the front doors. According to feng shui principles, this arrangement meant that money was "flowing out." After the desk was moved and the doors repositioned, the hotel became packed with guests!

Above: **Lion dances are often performed when shops or businesses first open. Owners hope the dances will bring good luck to their new venture.**

Wayang Performances

Wayang is the Malay word for a dramatic performance and is used to describe Chinese street opera. Wayang is the legacy of a rich cultural tradition that took root in Singapore's immigrant society about 150 years ago. Although Singapore is very modern, this art form is still popular today.

Music is an important part of the performance. The opera is accompanied by a two-part orchestra. It consists of *wen* (WUHN), or civil, music and *wu* (WOO), or military, music. Wen music is played by string and wind instruments, while wu music makes use of drums, cymbals, and gongs. The opera themes are usually taken from Chinese literary classics or history, with an emphasis on a moral message, such as justice, patriotism, and loyalty to family. The performers use mime techniques with few props and wear elaborate and colorful costumes and headdresses — the more elaborate the costume, the more important the performer. The colors of the robes represent certain personality traits. For example, a character in a red or gold robe is supposed to be loyal, brave, and generous.

Below: **Chinese opera is gaining a wider following in Singapore. This performer is giving a demonstration of this ancient art form.**

A Brief History

Chinese opera flourished in Singapore in the late nineteenth and early twentieth centuries as open-air entertainment for the masses. Wayang continued to thrive during the Japanese occupation of Singapore between 1942 and 1945. At that time, Western forms of culture and entertainment were banned. Interest in Chinese opera declined in the 1950s, when movies, variety shows, and band concerts became popular. In the late 1960s, professional theater declined, but amateur groups rekindled interest in wayang as they adjusted to the demands of the younger generation with innovative props.

Chinese opera is still very popular in Singapore. The older generation enjoys the entertainment, while the younger generation appreciates it as an art form. Operas are often performed to glorify deities or to appease the restless souls of the dead during the month of the "hungry ghosts" in August, when many Chinese believe the souls of the dead are released from their resting place to look for food and pleasure.

Above: **Facial make-up in Chinese opera is used to give an indication of the character's traits.**

71

Women in Singapore

The women who came from China to Singapore in the 1930s are often called "the mothers of Singapore." They married the male migrant workers who populated the country and helped create a stable environment for Singaporeans today.

In the 1930s, Singapore was full of single Chinese men who smoked opium, gambled, and got into fights. These men only planned to stay in Singapore until they became rich. After that, they intended to return to China.

During this time, the British government in Singapore began to restrict male immigration to the country due to the lack of jobs. The immigration of women, however, was not restricted. Many women came to Singapore, where they married Chinese laborers and raised families. Most of Singapore's Chinese citizens can trace their links to the country from this time.

Despite the influx of female immigrants, however, Singapore remained a male-oriented society, and women did not have much status except as wives and mothers. Some men even had two wives. Several outstanding women fought the discrimination. Elizabeth Choy and Shirin Fozdar (1905–92) helped establish the Singapore Council of Women (SCW) in 1951. SCW fought for

Above: **In 1994, Justice Lai Siu Chiu became the first woman in Singapore to be appointed to the Supreme Court Bench.**

Below: **Chan Choy Siong (*standing*) fought for women's rights in Singapore and played a large role in passing the Women's Charter.**

basic women's rights in marriage, work, and education. The Women's Charter was passed by Parliament in 1961. This charter gave women equal marital and legal status as men. After the charter was passed, SCW lacked a uniting cause and was disbanded in 1971. Its spiritual successor, the Singapore Council of Women's Organizations (SCWO), was formed in 1980.

Today, SCWO represents thirty-eight affiliated organizations and has more than 95,000 members. These organizations seek to help women through community-based service groups and by trying to influence national policies.

Some internationally known Singaporean women are Jaya Mohideen, ambassador to Belgium; Chan Heng Chee, ambassador to the United States; Noeleen Heyzer, executive director of the United Nations Development Fund for Women; and Ailine Wong, senior minister of education.

Unfortunately, some discrimination still exists in wages, education, and citizenship for spouses and children. Despite these setbacks, about 56 percent of Singaporean women are part of the workforce.

Above: **Singaporean women are a powerful force in the workplace and make important contributions to the country's economy.**

SPREADING AWARENESS

The Association of Women for Action and Research (AWARE) was founded in 1985 to promote women and to address issues that affect women's lives. Lena Lim U Wen is the founding president. She is also the managing director of Select Books, a bookstore and publishing house that specializes in Southeast Asian books.

RELATIONS WITH NORTH AMERICA

Singapore and North America share extremely close economic and political ties. The United States is Singapore's most important economic partner. It is the largest market for Singapore's exports as well as being Singapore's third largest source of imports. The United States is also the largest source of foreign investment in Singapore. Both North America and Singapore share common trade interests and believe that free trade and open shipping lanes are mutually beneficial.

Opposite: **North American food and beverage chains, such as Planet Hollywood, have become commonplace in Singapore.**

Ties between North America and Singapore grow stronger every year. Singapore is currently negotiating a free trade agreement (FTA) with the United States and Canada, which will make it easier for the three countries to trade with one another. Many North American corporations, such as Microsoft and IBM, also have regional offices in Singapore.

Singapore's close ties with North America are not limited to business and politics, however. Many North Americans also live and work in Singapore. In fact, more than 26,000 North Americans currently make their home on the island.

Above: **The rumble of Harley-Davidson motorcycles is an increasingly common sound on the streets of Singapore.**

Historical Ties

Americans traded in Singapore as early as the 1790s. They were well-liked by locals because they were fair traders and were willing to sell modern weapons. The major European powers disapproved of these sales, however, and the Americans were banned from trading with Singapore until 1840. Their ships had to anchor at the nearby Riau islands. When Joseph Balestier was appointed the first American Consul to Singapore in 1834, he had to work from these islands for several years until he was allowed to set up his office in Singapore.

Balestier was married to Maria Revere, the daughter of Paul Revere, the American Revolutionary War hero. Paul Revere was a noted craftsman in silver and other metals, and he designed a bell for Saint Andrew's Cathedral in Singapore. This bell rang daily from the cathedral from 1843 until 1889. It is now on display at the U.S. Embassy in Singapore and is the only Revere bell outside the United States.

American missionaries began serving in Singapore as early as the 1840s. The American Methodist Mission established schools for Asians on the island. By 1915, the Methodists were operating seven schools in Singapore. Some of the country's premier schools today, such as Anglo-Chinese School and Methodist Girls School, trace their origins to American mission efforts.

World Wars

During World War I, when British troops left Singapore to fight in Europe, Americans living in Singapore joined the country's volunteer defense forces. During World War II, trade between Singapore and the United States helped finance Britain's war efforts. Buying goods from Singapore in U.S. dollars gave the British the money to buy war materials from the United States. This plan was sometimes called Britain's "dollar arsenal."

After the fall of Singapore, about one hundred American soldiers were interned in Changi Prison. A book and movie about an American imprisoned at Changi, titled *King Rat*, describe how he and his fellow prisoners suffered in the terrible conditions.

In the decades after World War II, U.S. ties with Singapore grew, especially after Singapore gained independence. Today, the United States has replaced Britain as Singapore's largest export market and the country's most important source of investment.

BUSINESS PIONEERS

As business and trade grew in the early twentieth century, a number of American companies set up regional bases in Singapore. Goodyear, Citibank, Esso, Mobil, and Kodak (*above*) are some American companies whose ties with Singapore are almost a century old.

Opposite: St. Andrew's Cathedral in Singapore once used a bell designed by Paul Revere. Today, the bell is displayed at the U.S. Embassy in Singapore as a symbol of the long relationship between the two countries.

Political and Economic Ties

Since gaining independence in 1965, Singapore has worked closely with the United States. Singapore's strong anticommunist stand made it an important ally during the Cold War. Singapore was also a supply center for U.S. troops during the Vietnam War.

In the post-Cold War era, Singapore, the United States, and Canada have shared common goals in promoting international cooperation and free trade. The United States and Singapore are both members of the Asia-Pacific Economic Cooperation (APEC). Singapore has also been instrumental in promoting the annual dialogue between the United States and the Association of Southeast Asian Nations (ASEAN). Singapore and Canada have close ties through their strong commitment to the Commonwealth of Nations and the programs it carries out.

Above: **Canadian prime minister Jean Chretien (*left*) and Singaporean prime minister Goh Chok Tong (*right*) discussed bilateral issues at an official dinner in Singapore in 1998.**

Business to Business

Singapore imposes very low import duties and taxes; as a result, many North American companies have established manufacturing and services-related businesses in the country, as well as finance and business centers. The country is a natural regional hub for economic interests in Southeast Asia because it is at the crossroads of international trade. Many North American corporations have found that locating in Singapore gives them access to both local and regional business. In fact, Singapore was voted the world's best business destination in 2000 by *Business Traveler Asia Pacific*, a regional monthly publication. The ranking was based on safety, cleanliness, ease of doing business and getting around, and prices. Singapore has also been ranked among the top convention cities in the world.

Ties between Singaporean and U.S. companies are strong. For example, Singapore-based Creative Technology Limited makes digital audio equipment, such as sound cards for computers. This company works closely with Microsoft Corporation in the United States to ensure its products are compatible with Microsoft's Windows operating system.

In 1999, the U.S. Embassy and the American Chamber of Commerce launched the SesaME business opportunity program. The objective of this program is to promote joint ventures between U.S. and Singaporean small and medium-sized enterprises (SMEs).

Opposite: **In 1985, Senior Minister Lee Kuan Yew (*front row*) addressed a joint session of the U.S. Congress on free trade.**

Above: **Lee Kuan Yew (*second from right*), prime minister of Singapore, visits the USS *Ranger* in 1989.**

Military Ties

Singapore enjoys close military ties with the United States and Canada. Singapore believes that a strong U.S. military presence is important to maintain stability in the region. Singapore buys many of its weapons and military aircraft, such as F-16 fighters and AH-64 attack helicopters, from the United States.

Singapore provides ship repair and supply facilities for the U.S. Navy, which keeps a small, permanent support group on the island. Small detachments of U.S. fighter aircraft also deploy regularly to Singapore for exercises. The two countries participate in numerous joint exercises, including the Cooperation Afloat Readiness and Training (CARAT), which is a series of exercises between the U.S. and Southeast Asian navies.

Singapore's close military ties with the United States also have economic benefits. For example, in 1984, Singaporean and U.S. engineers began working on a program to install a more powerful engine in Singapore's A-4 attack aircraft. The program provided a tremendous boost to Singapore's high-technology industries.

Singapore is also in the final round of discussions to join the NATO Flying Training in Canada (NFTC) program. By taking part in this program, The Republic of Singapore Air Force (RSAF) will be able to send six pilots a year for a twenty-year period to attend advanced flying training courses at Canadian bases.

Overcoming Obstacles

Although ties between North America and Singapore have always been strong, relations between Singapore and the United States have sometimes been strained.

At times, the United States has angered the Singaporean government by commenting on Singapore's domestic affairs. In 1988, Hank Hendrickson, then the first secretary at the U.S. Embassy in Singapore, was expelled from the country after the Singaporean government accused him of helping political parties opposed to the PAP. In the 1990s, an American teenager, Michael Fay, was arrested for vandalism. The eighteen-year-old was sentenced to caning and a four-month jail sentence. This sentence caused friction between the Singaporean and U.S. governments because the U.S. government felt the punishment was too severe.

The United States and Singapore have also disagreed over freedom of the press. Certain U.S. publications, such as *Time* magazine and *Asian Wall Street Journal,* have published articles that have criticized Singapore. As a result, these journals have occasionally had their circulations restricted in Singapore.

Below: **Singapore's prime minister Goh Chok Tong (*right*) greets then U.S. Secretary of State Madeleine Albright (*left*). Despite occasional setbacks, the United States and Singapore have very strong ties.**

Education

About four thousand Singaporeans attend college in the United States every year. The U.S. Education Information Center (USEIC) provides Singaporeans interested in studying in the United States with up-to-date information on all U.S. universities. Many of Singapore's leaders have studied in the United States, including Singapore's prime minister, Goh Chok Tong, who received his master's degree from Williams College in Massachusetts.

Singaporeans who have obtained Fulbright scholarships study and conduct research in the United States. The Fulbright Program aims to increase understanding between U.S. citizens and those of other countries. Just over two hundred Singaporeans have participated in the program since it began in 1946. Many North American Fulbright scholars conduct research on regional issues at the Institute of Southeast Asian Studies in Singapore.

Overseas Ties

Organizations such as Contact Singapore in Boston and Club Singapore Toronto help Singaporeans in North America stay up-to-date with the latest news from home. These organizations also teach North Americans about Singapore and help develop stronger ties between East and West.

Left: **Many North American families live in Singapore. This young American girl is enjoying a tennis lesson at the American Club in Singapore.**

Research

Higher education and medical facilities are top priorities in Singapore, and the country's Economic Development Board (EDB) encourages Western universities to work with local institutions. In the late 1990s, Johns Hopkins Medicine (JHM) set up a research center with the National University of Singapore and Singapore's National University Hospital. Current projects include cancer research and diagnosis.

The Terry Fox Run

The Terry Fox Run is an annual charity event held in Singapore and many other countries to raise funds for cancer research. The very first Terry Fox Run was held in Canada in 1981 to honor the memory of Canadian Terry Fox. In 1980, after losing his right leg to cancer, Fox attempted to run across Canada to raise funds for cancer research and increase awareness of cancer. Since then, the many Terry Fox Runs held all over the world have raised more than U.S. $250 million for cancer research.

Above: **The Terry Fox Run has captured the hearts of many Singaporeans who help raise funds for cancer research. This picture shows the start of the 2000 Terry Fox Run in Singapore.**

North Americans in Singapore

About eighteen thousand U.S. citizens and eight thousand Canadians currently live in Singapore. North American children attend either the Singapore American School or the Canadian International School, while adults work in many areas of the economy, including banking and information technology. North Americans also work at the National Institute of Education as consultants and teachers and at the Regional English Language Center (RELC), which offers degrees in linguistics and carries out regional research.

Many North Americans like living in Singapore and have a comfortable lifestyle there. Singapore has many retail chain stores that are familiar to North Americans, such as Borders and Starbucks. Grocery stores are packed with familiar brands, such as Betty Crocker, Pillsbury, and Nabisco. *USA Today* and other North American newspapers are sold at some newsstands. The Television Corporation of Singapore (TCS) also broadcasts many American shows, and cable television features American channels.

Below: **Canadian prime minister Jean Chretien (center) visited the Canadian High Commission staff and their family members in Singapore in 1998.**

Singaporeans in North America

Although many Singaporeans study and work in North America, few actually immigrate there. Most choose to return to Singapore after their studies or overseas attachments are completed because they have strong family ties in their country. Many retain strong links with Singapore when they are in the United States and celebrate special Singaporean occasions. For example, the Singapore National Day 2000 celebration, held at the Omni Los Angeles Hotel, was an excellent chance for Singaporeans to play host to their North American friends. Over 250 Americans and Singaporeans attended the event, including Chan Heng Chee, Singapore's ambassador to the United States.

Since relatively small numbers of Singaporeans immigrate to the United States, Singapore citizens are eligible for the U.S. Diversity Immigrant Visa Program. This program makes 55,000 permanent resident visas available each year to eligible applicants. To qualify for the program, an applicant must be from a country that has not sent more than 50,000 immigrants to the United States over a five-year period.

Above: People who work and study overseas often celebrate the special occasions of their native country. In this picture, an American student in Singapore celebrates Independence Day in her own special way.

Above: Tourists enjoy the tranquility of Singapore's Botanic Gardens.

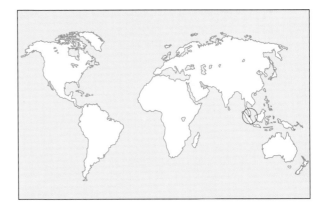

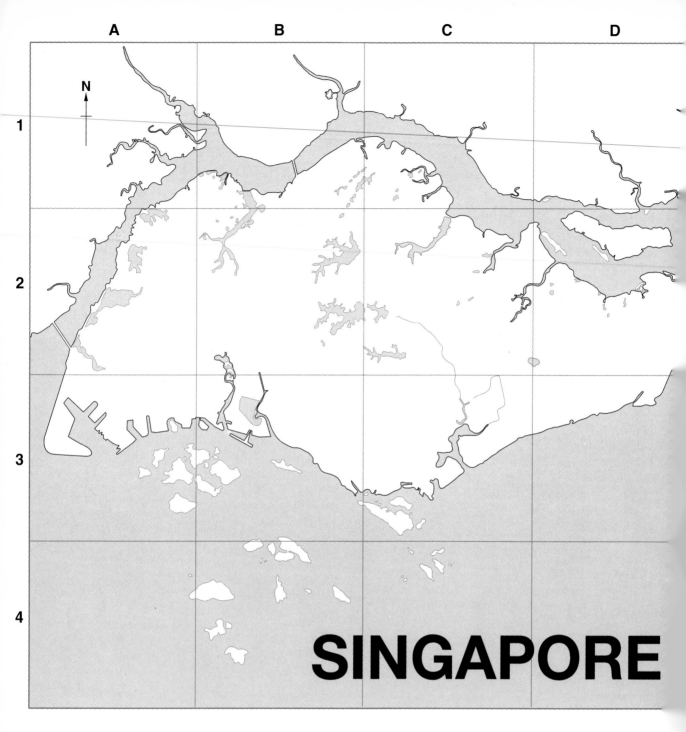

SINGAPORE

How Is Your Geography?

Learning to identify the main geographical areas and points of a country can be challenging. Although it may seem difficult at first to memorize the locations and spellings of major cities or the names of mountain ranges, rivers, deserts, lakes, and other prominent physical features, the end result of this effort can be very rewarding. Places you previously did not know existed will suddenly come to life when referred to in world news, whether in newspapers, television reports, or other books and reference sources. This knowledge will make you feel a bit closer to the rest of the world, with its fascinating variety of cultures and physical geography.

Used in a classroom setting, the instructor can make duplicates of this map using a copy machine. (PLEASE DO NOT WRITE IN THIS BOOK!) Students can then fill in any requested information on their individual map copies. Used one-on-one, the student can also make copies of the map on a copy machine and use them as a study tool. The student can practice identifying place names and geographical features on his or her own.

Above: **These Singaporeans are listening to a bird singing competition, a popular event among bird owners. Owners of winning birds receive prizes.**

Singapore at a Glance

Official Name	Republic of Singapore
Capital	Singapore
Official Languages	Mandarin (Chinese), English, Malay (also the national language), Tamil (Indian)
Population	4,151,264 (July 2000 estimate) *Note: About 1,000,000 of the population are not citizens or permanent residents of Singapore.*
Land Area	255 square miles (660 square km)
Highest Point	Bukit Timah Hill 545 feet (166 m)
Ethnic Groups	Chinese 77%, Malay 14%, Indian 7.6%, other 1.4%
Literacy Rate	91%
Major Religions	Buddhist, Christian, Confucianist, Hindu, Muslim
Important Holidays	Chinese New Year (January/February)
	Hari Raya Haji (March)
	National Day (August 9)
	Deepavali (October/November)
	Christmas (December 25)
	Hari Raya Puasa (December/January)
Important Leaders	Yusof bin Ishak (1910–1970)
	Lee Kuan Yew (1923–)
	David Saul Marshall (1908–1995)
National Anthem	"Majulah Singapura" ("Let Singapore Flourish")
Major Exports	Chemicals, machinery and equipment, mineral fuels
Major Imports	Chemicals, foodstuffs, machinery and equipment, mineral fuels
Currency	Singapore dollar (S$ 1.8 = U.S. $1 as of 2001)

Opposite: **These masks depict characters from Chinese mythology.**

Glossary

Mandarin (Chinese) Vocabulary

char kway teow (CHAH kway tee-ow): fried flat noodles.

chi (CHEE): energy.

Chingay (CHIN-gay): masquerade.

fa (FAH): prosperity.

feng shui (FUNG shway): Chinese geomancy.

gong xi fa cai (GOHNG see FAH chie): a Chinese New Year greeting.

hong bao (HUNG bough): a red envelope containing money that is given to loved ones at Chinese New Year.

mee (ME): yellow wheat noodles.

wen (WUHN): civil opera music using strings and wind instruments.

wu (WOO): military opera music using percussion instruments.

Tamil (Indian) Vocabulary

Deepavali (dee-PAHV-ah-lee): Indian festival of lights celebrating the victory of good over evil.

kavadis (KAH-vah-dees): wooden or metal headdresses carried during the Hindu festival of Thaipusam.

raita (rye-EE-tah): yogurt mixed with cucumbers and herbs.

roti prata (ROH-tee PRAH-tah): a flat, traditional Indian pancake made from flour and usually served with curry.

Thaipusam (TIE-poo-sahm): Indian festival of human endurance and self-sacrifice.

Thimithi (TIH-mih-tee): Hindu fire-walking festival.

Vesak (VAY-sahk): a festival commemorating the birth of Buddha.

vindaloo (VIN-dah-loo): a fiery hot tomato and chicken or lamb stew.

Malay Vocabulary

akad nikah (AH-kahd NEE-kah): a verbal contract between a bridegroom and the bride's father.

Allah (AH-lah): Islamic term for God.

baba (BAH-bah): a male Peranakan.

haj (HAHJ): a Muslim pilgrimage.

Hari Raya Haji (HAH-ree RYE-ah HAHJ-jee): a Muslim festival that celebrates the pilgrimage to Mecca.

Hari Raya Puasa (HAH-ree RYE-ah PWAH-sah): a Muslim festival that celebrates the end of the fasting month.

kebaya (kuh-BYE-yah): long-sleeved tunic.

mas kahwin (MAHS KAH-win): a special gift.

nasi padang (NAH-see PAH-dahng): a rice buffet offering chicken, shrimp, and beef curries.

nonya (NYOH-nyah): a female Peranakan.

Orang Laut (OH-rahng LAH-oat): Singaporean sea gypsies.

Peranakans (puh-RAH-nah-KAHNS): people who are of mixed Malay and Straits Chinese ancestry.

Ramadan (RAH-mah-dahn): the Muslim holy month of fasting.

satay (SAH-tay): skewered meat grilled over charcoal.

sepak takraw (seh-PAHK TAHK-raw): a rattan ball game.

Singapura (SING-ah-POO-rah): Sanskrit word meaning "lion city."

Syariah (SHAH-ree-ah): Muslim religious law.

Temasek (tuh-MAH-sek): sea town.

temenggong (tuh-MUNG-gohng): a territorial chief.

wayang (WHY-yang): Chinese street opera.

English Vocabulary

arable: fit for crop production.

archaeological: relating to the study of ancient peoples.

banana money: paper money printed by the Japanese during World War II.

city-state: an independent state consisting of a city and its surrounding territory.

curry: spicy Indian or Malay stew.

dialect: a variety of a language that differs from the standard language used.

diorama: a life-size exhibit displaying realistic sculpted figures in lifelike, detailed surroundings.

diversified: increased the variety of products, investments, etc., to provide a more balanced economic plan.

durian: a highly pungent Asian fruit.

embankment: a raised structure or land formation that serves to hold back water.

gantry: a raised frame structure that conveys signals or other information.

geomancy: the art of establishing a harmonious, energetic interaction between a person and place by placing the objects and structures in the person's surroundings to allow the flow of positive energy, thus achieving physical and spiritual harmony.

hub: a center of activity; a centralized position or routing center.

immigrant: a person who moves to a country and settles there.

indigenous: originating in or characteristic of a particular region or country.

infrastructure: bridges, roads, and other basic facilities serving a country.

innovative: characterized by change or the introduction of something new.

intern: put in jail; imprison.

laterization: the sinking of nutrients far below the soil's surface.

mangrove: tropical tree with large, dense prop roots that help hold soil together.

migrate: to move from one place or region to another, in search of shelter, work, or food.

mobilize: put in a state of readiness.

monsoons: seasons in southern Asia characterized by long periods of heavy rainfall.

negotiate: confer in order to reach an agreement.

peninsula: land surrounded by water on three sides.

pilgrimage: journey to a sacred place.

polytechnic: a school that concentrates on technical arts and applied sciences.

reclamation: the act of recovering, restoring, or reclaiming.

sabotage: to deliberately destroy, damage, or hinder, usually as part of a war effort against enemy resources.

shroud: cover; hide from view.

simulated: made to look genuine or natural.

strait: narrow passage of water.

sultan: ruler.

More Books to Read

Diary of a Girl in Changi 1941–1945. Sheila Allan (Seven Hills)
Exciting Singapore: A Visual Journey. Exciting Asia series. David Blocksidge
    (Periplus Editions)
The Food of Singapore: Authentic Recipes from the Manhattan of the East. Food of series.
    Djoko Wibisono (Charles E. Tuttle)
Passport Singapore: Your Pocket Guide to Singaporean Business, Customs & Etiquette.
    Alexandra Kett and Jane E. Lasky (World Trade Press)
A Photographic Guide to Birds of Peninsular Malaysia and Singapore. G. W. H. Davison
    (Chelsea Green)
Singapore. Cultures of the World series. Lesley Layton (Benchmark Books)
Singapore. Enchantment of the World series. Marion Marsha Brown (Children's Press)
Singapore: City of Gardens. William Warren (Charles E. Tuttle)
Singapore Sketchbook: The Restoration of a City. Gretchen Liu (Tuttle Publishing)
Singular Stories: Tales from Singapore. Robert Yeo, ed. (Lynne Rienner Publishers)

Videos

Fodor's Video: Singapore. (IVN Entertainment)
Singapore. (Education 2000)
Singapore: Crossroads of Asia. (Video Visits)

Web Sites

lcweb2.loc.gov / frd / cs / sgtoc.html
library.thinkquest.org / 12405 / index.html
www.museum.org.sg / discover_heritage / heritagekids / Hkids.shtml /
www.sg / kids
www.singapore-ca.com

Due to the dynamic nature of the Internet, some web sites stay current longer than
others. To find additional web sites, use a reliable search engine with one or more of
the following keywords to help you locate information about Singapore. Keywords:
Bukit Timah, Changi, Lee Kuan Yew, merlion, Sir Stamford Raffles, Sentosa, Singapore River.

Index